REBECCA PARKINSON

12
Hidden
Heroes

Bible people
who did BRAVE
THINGS for God

OT

DayOne

© Day One Publications 2010

First printed 2010

ISBN 978-1-84625-210-5

Scripture quotations taken from the
HOLY BIBLE, NEW INTERNATIONAL VERSION.

Copyright © 1973, 1978, 1984 by International Bible Society.

Used by permission of Hodder & Stoughton Publishers,
A member of the Hodder Headline Group.
All rights reserved.

"NIV" is a registered trademark of
International Bible Society.
UK trademark number 1448790.

British Library Cataloguing in Publication Data available

Published by Day One Publications
Ryelands Road, Leominster, HR6 8NZ

TEL 01568 613 740 FAX 01568 611 473

email—sales@dayone.co.uk

UK web site—www.dayone.co.uk

USA web site—www.dayonebookstore.com

Designed by **documen**
Printed by Thomson Litho, East Kilbride

Dedication

For my parents in the year of their Golden Wedding.
Thank you for all your love, support and encouragement
throughout my life.

Contents

Keeping a careful watch

The story of Miriam

1

(This story is based on Exodus 2:1–10.)

Miriam carefully stirred the pan of stew bubbling on the open fire. She hummed quietly to herself, hoping to block out the sound of her parents' anxious voices. She knew what they were discussing. The same conversation had been repeated day after day for weeks now; today, though, there seemed to be a fresh urgency in their voices.

Needing reassurance, Miriam tiptoed over and sat down next to her father, resting her head gently on his shoulder.

'The time has come,' he whispered sadly. 'He must go.'

Miriam jumped up. 'No!' she screamed. 'It's not fair!'

'Miriam,' scolded her mother. 'Sit down and don't make a fuss. We have kept this secret long enough. We mustn't spoil things now.'

Hurriedly, Miriam sat down. The last thing she wanted to do was to ruin all those months of secrets.

'May I hold him?' she asked softly.

Her mother looked down at the little bundle in her arms and nodded. 'Try not to wake him,' she whispered. 'I'm tired and could do with some sleep. I seem to have done nothing but feed him for the last three months, just to keep him from crying.'

Miriam gently lifted the baby and carried him closer to the fire. In the flickering light she could see his soft black hair and long eyelashes. She slid her finger into his small hand and was glad when, in his sleep, he seemed to feel the need to tighten his grip. Her mind wandered over the events of the past year. First there was the terrible announcement by Pharaoh that all baby boys born to the Israelites had to be killed. Then the quiet announcement to the family that Miriam's mother was pregnant ... how they had prayed that the baby would be a girl! But it was not to be. A baby boy had arrived and the fight to keep him a secret had begun in earnest. Only the immediate family and a few close friends knew anything about the baby. How different it had been when Miriam and her brother Aaron had been born! Then, there had been huge celebrations; now, everyone was gripped with fear in case the baby was discovered. And yet her mother and father seemed quite convinced that God was in this somewhere. They felt that, somehow, God had a plan for this baby boy, and that God would protect his life. Miriam didn't know about that! All she knew, as she gazed at his tiny face, was that she would do anything to keep her tiny brother safe.

Morning came too quickly. Miriam was woken early by her father.

'Miriam,' he spoke in an urgent tone, 'Miriam, the time has come. You must hurry before everyone in the town is awake. Take the baby and hide him as we discussed. Then wait and see what happens. We'll wait here and pray that God will protect you both.'

Miriam scrambled out of bed and pulled on her clothes. Her mother sadly handed her a basket.

'Go quickly,' said her mother. 'And may God be with you.'

It didn't take long for Miriam to sneak along the quiet path to the river Nile. She glanced around nervously. She could see no one. Quickly, she parted the bulrushes and placed the basket on the water. She folded back the cloth that was covering the baby and kissed him gently on the head.

'Goodbye, little one,' she said softly. 'May God protect you. I will be close by to see what happens to you.'

She pulled the curtain of bulrushes round to cover the basket and ran to hide in some trees a short distance away.

To Miriam it seemed as if she was forever waiting, keeping watch. Her mind was full of questions. What if the basket had sunk? What if the basket had floated away?

She was just preparing to go and check when two noises made her jump. She pressed herself firmly against the trees in the hope that she would be less visible. First there was the sound of talking. Two ladies, she thought. Who were they? Were they Israelites—or maybe the enemy? Then the noise of crying filled the air. The baby was awake!

The ladies came into view and Miriam froze. She recognized one of them. She had seen her many times, dressed in ornate clothes, parading through the town alongside Pharaoh. Pharaoh's daughter!

What should she do? Miriam's mind was whirling. Who could be a worse person to find an Israelite baby? Surely only Pharaoh himself! She kept watching, wondering if she should run forward and grab the baby and try to escape. But if Pharaoh found out who this baby belonged to, everyone who knew about him would be punished. So she remained still.

Pharaoh's daughter approached the water. She looked around, puzzled.

'Where's that crying coming from?' she asked her servant.

The servant-girl shook her head. 'It seems to be coming from the water,' she answered, moving towards the sound.

Miriam held her breath.

The servant-girl parted the bulrushes and reached forwards, pulling the basket out of the water. She set it down in front of Pharaoh's daughter and folded back the cloth.

'I think this must be one of the Israelite babies,' said Pharaoh's daughter. 'Look at the tiny little thing! Lift him out. Let's see if we can stop him crying.'

She carefully took the baby from her servant and rocked him gently in her arms.

'He can't be killed,' she whispered. 'We've rescued him from the water. We'll call him Moses, and he will be my child. My father won't mind if I demand it. He says I can have whatever I like.'

She turned to the servant-girl. 'You'll have to find me someone to feed the child,' she ordered. 'An Israelite woman would be the best.'

From her hiding-place, Miriam could hardly believe what she was hearing. She smoothed out her clothes and stepped out onto the path, pretending she was taking an early-morning stroll.

'Excuse me,' she said politely. 'I couldn't help overhearing that you would like someone to nurse this baby for you. My mum would do it for you, if you wanted her to.'

Pharaoh's daughter nodded. 'I would like that,' she said. 'I'll pay your mother, and she can bring the boy to the palace when he is older and can eat proper food. I would like him to visit regularly.'

Miriam nodded and picked up the basket. She couldn't believe it!

As soon as Miriam was out of sight of Pharaoh's daughter, she began to run. What would her mother and father say? Surely God had protected all the family in the way her parents had said he would!

She threw open the door.

'Mum!' she yelled. 'Mum, come here now!'

Her mother ran into the room. At first, she looked horrified when she saw the basket. 'Miriam!' she scolded. 'Oh Miriam, why have you brought him back? Has anyone seen you?'

'No, Mum,' said Miriam, laughing. 'You don't understand! God has protected him just as you said he would! And better than that ...'

Miriam spilled out the whole story, which was met with gasps of astonishment and tears. When she had finished, her father rose slowly to his feet.

'We believed this child was special,' he said in a voice full of wonder. 'God has saved him. He will be with us through his young life so that we can teach him to follow our God. He will then live in the palace of Pharaoh. Who knows what amazing plan God has in store for him! I believe that Moses has been born for a very special reason.'

Moses was brought up to follow the ways of the Israelite people. When he was old enough, he moved to the palace of Pharaoh and learned to read and write alongside other Egyptians. Eventually, it was Moses who led the people of Israel out of slavery in Egypt. Many people know the stories of Moses and the burning bush, the parting of the Red Sea, and the Ten Commandments. Moses became one of the best-known and best-loved characters in the Bible, but little is known about Miriam. She is mentioned again in Exodus chapter 15, when she joins Moses in a song to celebrate the escape of the Israelites from Egypt, but even then it is only a brief mention. I wonder what would have happened if Miriam hadn't stayed and kept watch over her baby brother? The life of Moses would certainly have been very different, and he may well have not been able to do the things that he did.

Miriam is a hidden hero of the Bible. What she did may not have been as dramatic as the things Moses did, but without her, the story could not have unfolded in the way it did. She did a small job, simply watching over her baby brother, but that was a vital part of the plan that God had for Moses' life and for the people of Israel.

As we grow up, we can often be asked to do little tasks that seem boring or unimportant. It is good to remember that the small things we do are part of the bigger plan that God has for our lives and for the lives of other people.

What do you think?

1. What do you think could have happened if Miriam hadn't kept watch over her brother?

2. Why was it important that Moses was brought up as part of an Israelite family?

3. What can we learn from Miriam?

Dare to be different!

The story of Caleb

2

*(This story is based on
Numbers chapters 13–14
and Joshua chapter 14.)*

C aleb walked briskly back to his tent, keeping his head down to avoid the glares of the people who were crying as he passed. He had never been so angry. Angry and stunned at the same time! How could the people of Israel not realize that their God was powerful enough to do absolutely anything? He had rescued them from the land of Egypt; parted the Red Sea so they could walk through on dry land; fed them in an amazing way with special bread from heaven; and done hundreds of other miracles to show them that he loved them and would always protect them. And still they didn't believe! Caleb threw back the canvas tent door and marched inside.

'I've done my best!' he muttered to himself. 'We could easily win with God on our side!'

Caleb glanced around the tent. Earlier that day he had been so glad to arrive home. Forty days of being away from his family was a long time, but he had felt privileged to be asked to carry out such an important task. He remembered when their leader Moses had first called the Israelites together and announced the names of the men who were to go as spies into the neighbouring towns and cities. Twelve of them were chosen, one man from each of the tribes of Israel. They were to spend forty days exploring the area before the army moved in to take the land for themselves. God had promised this land to the Israelites many years before, and Caleb was very excited at the thought of watching God keep his promise.

'And now I'll have to wait for years,' he fumed through gritted teeth. He closed his eyes and let his mind wander back over the past few weeks.

'God has chosen you,' said Moses, the leader of the Israelites, to the twelve spies before they set off. 'You are to explore the whole land. I want to know what the land is like, what the people are like, whether the cities are well protected, and whether the land produces good crops. If possible, bring back some food with you so we can all see for ourselves that what you tell us is true.'

At first, all twelve of the men had been enthusiastic. They had moved from place to place trying their best not to make the local people suspicious of them, taking note of everything that Moses had asked them to look for. It had been surprising to see how well fortified some of the cities were. Some had huge, thick walls; some had large, strong armies. In some cities the people were so tall they were like giants! A few of the other spies had been worried, but Caleb and his friend Joshua had kept reminding them that God was stronger than anything they had seen. Together they had collected lots of fruit to take back to show the Israelites. In one town they had cut down such a large bunch of grapes that it had taken two men to carry it, on a stick resting between their shoulders!

When they arrived back at the camp, Moses had called all the Israelites together. Caleb had found it hard to control his excitement; at last, God was about to keep his promise! He stood with the other spies in front of the crowds. One after the other, they told of the beautiful land they had visited. They described the food and drink and showed the produce they had collected. They talked of the huge cities with their strong fortifications and of the size of the people who lived there. Caleb waited impatiently for his turn. Eventually, Moses nodded to him.

Caleb had taken a deep breath, allowing his voice to boom out, ready to rouse the people to action.

'We should go immediately and take the land for ourselves!' he shouted, raising his fist in the air. 'With God on our side, we can certainly do it!'

He had waited for the roar of the crowd, the loud cheer that said the people knew God could do anything. But all he heard was another spy's voice.

'We must not attack this land,' the voice whined. 'These people are stronger than we are. We will definitely lose.'

At once, all the crowd had starting grumbling and complaining. Ten of the spies began to tell frightening stories about the armies they had seen and how impossible it would be ever to win against such strength. Caleb and Joshua had tried to calm the people down, but it was no use. The complaints grew louder and louder.

'Why didn't you just leave us to die in Egypt rather than bringing us out here where a foreign army will destroy us?' one man bellowed in the direction of Moses.

'These armies will take our wives and children away from us,' shouted another.

'Why don't we choose a new leader and go back and live in Egypt?' an angry voice called. 'I'd rather be a slave than be here!'

Caleb couldn't believe what he heard. He remembered how dreadful it had been in Egypt. He remembered the beatings, the lack of food, the endless painful work. How could the Israelites have forgotten the wonderful way God had rescued them and brought them safely to this point?

Caleb glanced over to Moses, their leader. He had fallen to the ground, face down, obviously deeply upset by what was happening. Caleb then looked at Joshua. He was relieved that at least he showed the same look of complete astonishment that Caleb felt must be written all over his own face.

Caleb had tried to talk to the people again.

'Please listen,' he begged. 'The land we saw is wonderful. We have nothing to fear. God has promised to give this land to us, and he always keeps his promises.'

It was no use. The people had become more and more angry. Then, suddenly, everyone's attention was turned towards the special tent—the Tent of Meeting, as they called it. The tent was positioned outside the main Israelite camp, and if there were ever any important decisions to be made, Moses would go to the tent and God would talk to him. Usually a pillar of cloud would appear when God was talking, but this time it was different! This time the whole tent seemed to fill up with the glory of God! Moses hurried to speak with God, and when he had reappeared that morning he had looked tired and sad.

'God is not pleased,' he announced to the Israelites. 'He asked how it could be possible that you still do not believe in him after all that he has done for you. He was so angry that I had to plead with him to continue to love you and not to give up caring for you. But I have bad news. For the next forty years you will all live here in the desert. You will wander from place to place with no land to call your own. After forty years God will bring you back to this place and will then keep his promise to you, as he always does. However, by the end of forty years, only Caleb and Joshua and all the children and young people who are now under the age of twenty will still be alive. The rest of you will never see the beautiful place that God so badly wanted you to have.'

Caleb opened his eyes. He could hear the people still sobbing outside. That made him even more cross. Why had they been so silly? It was too late. God had spoken, and now he would have to wait forty years to see God's promise fulfilled! Caleb shrugged his shoulders.

'At least God knows that Joshua and I trusted him,' he sighed wearily. 'At least we know that one day we will see God lead us into the beautiful land that we visited.'

For forty years Caleb, Joshua and the people of Israel did wander in the desert. At the end of that time, God led them into the land of Canaan that Caleb and Joshua had once explored. By then, Joshua had taken over from Moses as the leader of the Israelites and Caleb was an old man. However, Caleb was still as fit and healthy as he had been when he first went as a spy to the land. At the age of eighty-five Caleb was given part of the land that God had promised for him and his family. For Caleb, that must have been a very special moment!

Many people have heard of Moses and Joshua, the great leaders of the Israelites, but not so many know the story of Caleb. Caleb is one of the Bible's hidden heroes. He stood up for what he knew to be right even though it made him unpopular. He also trusted God always to keep his promises, even when it appeared to be impossible. Sometimes it can be hard for us to stand up for what we know to be right. This story teaches us that it is right to stand up for what we believe even when it feels as if crowds of people are against us. It also teaches us that God loves us to trust him, and that he always keeps his promises, even though sometimes we have to wait a long time before we see it happen.

What do you think?

1. How do you think Caleb felt when he was given part of the Promised Land after waiting for so many years?

2. Why do you think God sometimes makes us wait a while before he answers our prayers?

3. Do you think Caleb would have minded that Joshua became the leader of the Israelites after Moses died?

Hide!

The story of Rahab

3

*(This story is based on
Joshua chapters 2–6.)*

*T*he blare of the trumpets echoed around the city.
Something strange was going on. For the past six
days, the Israelite army had marched once around Jericho
before retreating back to its campsite a short distance
away. Today was different. Already the army had completed
six circuits of the city, and it looked as though it would
complete a seventh. The noise was eerie: the sound of
marching feet and the continual blasting of the trumpets.

In houses all over Jericho, people waited in fear. They
knew the power of the Israelites. For weeks, no one had
entered or left Jericho. They were prisoners, with no way
of escape.

From her house in the city wall, Rahab could see the
army as it passed by. She checked again that the red cord
was firmly attached to her window and then turned to look
at her cramped room. All her family and friends were there,
huddled together, hoping that what Rahab had told them
was correct. She had no doubts, although she had been
surprised when everyone turned up at her home. There
were people there she hadn't seen for years. Funny how
people forget that they don't like you or your job when they
need help!

Her young nephew tugged on her tunic.

'Auntie Rahab, will you tell us a story?' he asked.
'Will you tell us again why that red cord is going to keep
us safe?'

Rahab nodded. Maybe it would keep their minds off the
happenings outside.

The children gathered round and the adults became
silent. This was their only hope, their only way out of the
disaster that they felt sure was about to happen.

'It was just an ordinary day,' Rahab began. 'I'd been mending some clothes and doing a bit of cleaning when there was a knock on the door. I opened it and found two men standing there. I could tell immediately that they were strangers to the city. I guessed they were Israelites. I'd heard so many stories about them: how their God had parted the Red Sea, and how their God always gave them victory in their battles. Somehow, when I saw those two men, I was certain that they were spies. I couldn't turn them away; I suppose I knew they had a powerful God with them. So I invited them inside.'

She paused for a moment as she remembered what happened next. She had been so frightened.

'Within minutes, I heard a commotion in the streets outside. Someone had spotted the spies and reported it to the king. He had sent soldiers to find them. They were everywhere! I hurried the men upstairs onto the roof and hid them underneath the flax that was drying there. Almost immediately there was a loud banging on my door. I ran to open it. The soldiers were there, right outside my door! I tried to look calm, but inside, my heart was pounding and my legs were shaking in fear.

'"Where are the spies?" they bellowed.

'"There were some men here," I answered quickly, "but I didn't know who they were. They left as it grew dark, but I don't know which way they went. Hurry, and you might catch up with them somewhere."

'Immediately the soldiers ran off, looking this way and that in the hope that the spies hadn't got far.' Rahab paused and laughed. 'They didn't have much chance of finding them as they were on my roof!'

Everyone giggled; the sound of the marching and the trumpets seemed to be getting louder and it was good to break the uneasy tension for a few seconds.

A child's voice broke in. 'Why did you hide them, though, Auntie Rahab,' he questioned, 'when they were about to come and destroy our city?'

Rahab was quiet for a moment.

'I think,' she answered thoughtfully, 'that I had come to believe that their God was real. I told them that the whole of Jericho was terrified of their army and that we had heard how the Israelites had won every battle they ever fought. I told them I believed that God would give the city of Jericho to them when they attacked. And then I asked them a favour.'

'To keep us all safe?' asked a small girl.

Rahab smiled and continued. 'That's right. I asked that, when they came back to attack the city, they would save me and my family from being hurt in the disaster. They agreed and told me that, if I hung this red cord out of my window when the army attacked, everyone in my house would be safe. So here we are! After that, I lowered the spies out of the window and down the outside of the wall on a rope. I assume they escaped back to camp—I didn't hear that anyone had been caught.'

She stopped her story. The noise of the trumpets was getting louder. A baby began to cry. Suddenly, the house began to shake as a loud shout echoed around the city. All the army of Israel were shouting at once. There was a deafening crash. People screamed. The walls trembled. Everyone dived for cover.

All of a sudden there was a knock at the door. Rahab

hurried to answer it. She recognized the two men waiting outside.

'Hurry!' they said. 'You must come quickly! We promised that you and your family would be safe. Follow us!'

Carefully, the men led Rahab and her family over the rubble of the city walls. They had kept their promise; no one in her home was hurt.

✕✕✕✕✕

From that time onwards, Rahab lived among the Israelites. Eventually, she married and had children of her own. If we follow Rahab's family tree through four generations, we find that she was the great-great-grandma of King David, who was famous for defeating the giant Goliath. If we follow Rahab's descendants still further, we discover that, eventually, Jesus became part of her family tree!

Rahab is one of the Bible's hidden heroes. If she had been found hiding the spies, she would have been severely punished; yet she was willing to risk everything to help work out God's plan. She was just an ordinary person who hid two men on her roof, but what she did made a huge difference. When we are young, we can think that the things we do are small and insignificant. Rahab's story tells us that God can use the small, ordinary things in our lives to help work out his big plans.

What do you think?

1. What do you think would have happened if Rahab hadn't been willing to hide the spies?

2. What stories do you think Rahab had heard to convince her that the Israelite God was the true God that she wanted to follow?

3. Have a look in Matthew chapter 1 at the family tree of Jesus. Can you find Rahab's name? What was her son's name? Can you find her son's name in Ruth chapter 4? (We will look at his story in our next chapter.)

4. Have a look at Hebrews chapter 11. Can you find Rahab's name listed with the names of lots of other people who showed that they really trusted God?

In the corn fields
The story of Boaz

4

*(This story is based on
the book of Ruth.)*

B oaz gazed across the field towards the young woman carefully collecting the unwanted stalks of barley that the harvesters had left behind. He had never seen her before and yet he couldn't take his eyes off her! There was something special in the way she moved, something strangely attractive in the way she spoke to those around her, something gripping in the way she looked! He wandered slowly over to the workers.

'Good to see you,' he greeted them, 'and may God be with you.'

The men smiled and shouted their greetings back to him. They all loved Boaz. He was known as a fair and honest businessman who looked after his workers well and went out of his way to help the poor. Anyone living nearby who couldn't afford much food was always welcome in Boaz's fields. If any stalks of barley fell to the ground as the workers cut them, they would be left where they fell so that the poor could gather them for themselves.

Boaz sidled round to the foreman, surprised that he felt so embarrassed.

'You don't happen to know who that young lady over there is, do you?' he asked quietly, trying his best to sound uninterested.

The foreman carefully hid a smile.

'I do, actually,' he replied. 'Her name is Ruth. She's the one who came all the way back from her home-town to look after her mother-in-law, Naomi. She asked if it would be OK to gather some barley from the field today, and we said it would be fine. She's worked non-stop all morning except for one small break when the sun was too hot.'

Boaz felt his heart leap. So this was the Ruth that so

many people had talked about; the young woman who had given up so much to care for Naomi. Suddenly Boaz felt a glimmer of hope deep down inside him. He tried to blot it out. He was getting older; he mustn't build up his hopes. Slowly he walked over to Ruth at the edge of the field.

'Hello,' he said gently, hoping that his voice remained calm.

Ruth looked up, rather afraid to see the owner of the field peering down at her. She opened her mouth to speak, eager to explain that she had asked permission to be there, but Boaz spoke first.

'Don't be afraid,' he said kindly. 'You can gather barley from my fields any time you want. I have told the workers to look after you, and if you are thirsty in this heat then please go and help yourself to water from the jars over there.'

Ruth couldn't believe what she was hearing!

'Thank you, sir,' she stuttered. 'But why are you being so kind to me? I'm not even from round here. I'm a foreigner, and there's no reason why you should allow me into your field.'

Boaz smiled at her; she obviously didn't know his history! In his earlier days he too had often been treated like a stranger. When his father had married his mother, Rahab, many people hadn't approved of the marriage. Sometimes it had been hard for the family, but over the years they had proved that God had the power to change people's lives and they had become well loved and respected.

'I've heard all about you,' he answered softly. 'I know that a family used to live here in Bethlehem: Elimelech and

Naomi and their two sons. I know that they left Bethlehem to avoid the terrible famine and that they moved to Moab. I know that you married one of the sons but then all the men died, leaving you all alone. I also know that, in a deed of great kindness, you left your mum and dad in Moab and came all the way back here to Bethlehem, even though you would not know anybody and would probably be lonely. I believe you did all this simply to care for an old woman, and I know for certain that the God whom you have come to trust will look after you for your kindness.'

Ruth could hardly believe what Boaz was saying.

'Thank you,' she whispered. 'Thank you for being kind to me even though I am less important than any of your servants.'

Ruth continued to collect barley in the field all day. When it was mealtime Boaz invited her to sit with the workers and share his food. She ate until she was full and then wrapped up the leftovers to take home for Naomi to eat later. As she went back to work, Boaz ordered the men to drop extra barley on the ground near Ruth to make sure there was plenty for her to collect.

As darkness fell, Ruth staggered home and placed the crops she had collected in front of Naomi.

'Where did you get all that?' Naomi gasped, shaking her head in disbelief. 'Someone has been very kind to allow you to collect such a lot.'

'I've spent the whole day in the same field,' Ruth answered. 'The boss said I could go whenever I wanted, and he even shared his food with me!'

Ruth reached into her pocket and gave Naomi the small packet of roasted corn. 'Here, I saved the rest for you.'

Naomi took the food gratefully. 'Who was this man?' she asked. 'Do you know his name?'

'I do,' smiled Ruth. 'His name is Boaz.'

'Boaz!' Ruth jumped at Naomi's reaction.

'Boaz!' Naomi screeched again. 'God has been good to us! Boaz is one of our close relatives. In fact, round here we'd call him our "kinsman-redeemer", which means that, if we needed to, we could ask him to buy back the plot of land that once belonged to my husband, Elimelech.' She paused for a moment, then spoke with a twinkle in her eyes. 'Our law also means that we could even ask him to marry you!'

'Well, I don't know that he would want to do that,' laughed Ruth. 'But at least I can go and gather grain whenever we need it, so we won't stave!'

Day after day, Boaz went out into his fields in the hope that Ruth would be there. He would watch her cautiously, not wanting anyone to guess that he was falling in love! Ruth was so young and beautiful, he was certain she would never have time for him. Surely she would want a young husband, someone with whom she could have children and then grow old with.

One evening, towards the end of the harvest season, Boaz settled down to sleep on a rug near a pile of corn in his field. He loved to lie there in the darkness and gaze up at the beauty of the stars. It reminded him how huge the world was, and made him remember again that any problems he had were very small compared with the greatness of his God.

Suddenly, he heard a noise. He sat up, startled.

'Who's there?' he hissed into the darkness, his heart thudding inside his chest.

'It's me,' whispered a soft, unsure voice. 'Ruth, the one who's been gathering food in your field. Naomi sent me to find you to see if you would be willing to be a kinsman-redeemer for us.'

There was silence for a moment while Boaz tried to take in what he was hearing. He knew that for Ruth to approach him in this way meant that she wasn't only asking him to buy back their land, but was also agreeing to marry him if he wanted her!

'Ruth,' said Boaz in wonder, 'the more I get to know you, the kinder you seem to become! You could marry any rich, young man you wanted, but you are willing to marry me!'

In the darkness Ruth blushed slightly and looked down at the ground. She knew Boaz was older than she was, but during the past few months she had grown to love this important man who had shown her such care.

Boaz longed to leap up immediately and agree to everything Ruth wanted, but a terrible thought was spinning around in his head. He shut his eyes. What should he do? He had always been honest, always told the truth. Would it really matter if he didn't tell Ruth everything, especially as, if he did, everything might change?

He made a decision and opened his eyes. 'Ruth,' he said gently, 'I would love to do what you are asking. But I'm afraid that Naomi has a closer relative than me. I'm afraid that the law says that he has the first choice to buy back Elimelech's land ... and ...' he swallowed hard, '.. and ... the first choice of marrying you.'

Ruth's heart sank. She didn't want someone else; she wanted to marry Boaz.

'However,' Boaz continued, 'I have a plan! It may not work, but it's worth a try. I promise that I will sort it out today. Now you'd better go home to Naomi.'

Boaz sat at the town gate glancing anxiously up and down the road. It felt as though he had been waiting for hours! At last, he spotted the man he wanted. He hurried over.

'Come and sit over here, my friend,' he said. 'I want to ask you something.' The man followed.

Quickly Boaz asked ten of the town leaders to sit with them, so that they would hear exactly what was being discussed.

Boaz took a deep breath and addressed the man. 'You are the nearest relative of Elimelech, who died in the land of Moab. Naomi, Elimelech's widow, wants someone to buy the land that belonged to Elimelech. You have first choice. If you don't want the land, then I would like to buy it.'

The man spoke immediately. 'I'll buy it,' he said, eager to get more land for himself.

Boaz knew that now was the all-important moment. 'As soon as you buy the land,' he continued, 'you will also have to marry Ruth, the lady who came from Moab with Naomi.'

The man looked shocked. 'But I don't want another wife,' he said hurriedly. 'Especially not a foreign wife. No way! You can have the land and marry Ruth.'

Boaz felt as if he would burst with happiness. He hurried to tell Ruth the good news, and soon they were married. Before long, a baby was born. The baby was called Obed, and he filled the whole family with joy.

If we follow Boaz's family tree through three generations we find that he was the great-grandad of King David, who is famous for defeating the giant Goliath. If we follow Boaz's descendants still further, we discover that eventually Jesus became part of his family tree.

Many people have heard the story of Ruth and know her as a woman who loved God and cared for her mother-in-law, but Boaz is not so well known. Boaz is one of the Bible's hidden heroes. He was a good, fair boss who cared for the poor and for strangers and, in a beautiful way, that care led him to meet Ruth, his future wife. Not many of us will become rich and famous, but all of us have opportunities each day to care for other people, and God counts that as vitally important.

What do you think?

1. What do you think would have happened to Ruth and Naomi if Boaz had not cared for them?

2. Have a look through Matthew 1:1–6 and see if you can spot the names of Boaz and Ruth. Do you recognize any other names?

3. How do you think Naomi felt when her grandson was born? Have a look at Ruth 4:16–17 to help you.

A precious child
The story of Hannah

5

*(This story is based on
1 Samuel 1:1–2:26.)*

Hannah tried hard to smile, hoping that no one would see the pain she was feeling inside. She looked around at the children happily running about outside the tents, laughing and joking, playing hide-and-seek. It was good to see the delight on their faces and to hear their jokes. Children were a precious gift from God, she knew that, and it was up to God as to whom he gave such gifts to. She tried to swallow the lump in her throat. If only, she thought ... if only she could have a child.

She glanced over at Peninnah, who raised her eyes and smirked as if she knew how much Hannah would be struggling with this latest news. Why did she have to be so cruel? She already had lots of children, and now she was to have another! It was hard when your husband had two wives. Elkanah hadn't done anything wrong. Every man wanted to have children, and Hannah longed to have some of her own.

She got up quietly and moved inside the tent. At least here she would escape from Peninnah's mocking eyes. She sat down and began to sob. A gentle voice interrupted her crying.

'Hannah, Hannah, don't cry.' Her husband Elkanah stood beside her. 'Is it Peninnah? Have you heard her news?'

Hannah nodded, and Elkanah squeezed her shoulder.

'Don't be sad,' he whispered. 'You know I love you, whether you have children or not.'

Hannah looked up at his kind face. It was true. Elkanah did love her more than he loved Peninnah. Whenever he handed out food, he always gave Hannah more, and he always preferred to spend his time with Hannah rather than with his other wife. Unfortunately, that didn't stop the pain. All she wanted was a child.

It was almost time for the family to make the journey to Shiloh. They would travel there once a year to worship God. Eli the priest lived there in the temple. Each year, Hannah would go into the temple and cry out to God, pleading with him to give her a child. Each year, she went home disappointed, with the scoffing voice of Peninnah ringing in her ears. She began to pack. She would just have to cope with Peninnah. After all, Elkanah loved to go up to the temple; she must try to be happy for him.

Elkanah gazed sadly at Hannah. It broke his heart to see her like this. Every year was the same. It was as if the visit to the temple made things worse, as if here she understood even less why God would not allow her to have a child. She looked so pale and tired. He knew she hadn't eaten anything for days, but there was little he could do. Tomorrow, they would all travel back to Ramah, Peninnah would in time have her baby, and Hannah would cope as she always did. He went over to her.

'Hannah,' he said softly, 'Hannah, please eat something. Don't be sad. Don't I mean more to you than having ten sons?'

Hannah raised her eyes. She wished she could say yes. She loved Elkanah very much, but the truth was that she wanted a baby more than anything else in the world.

Hurriedly, she got to her feet. There was still time. They had eaten their evening meal and tomorrow they would go home; there was time to ask God just once more.

Quickly, she made her way to the temple. Eli, the priest,

was sitting on a chair by the door. She ran past him and threw herself on the floor.

'Lord,' she cried out to God, 'please don't forget me. Please give me a son. If you do, I will give him back to you for all the days of his life. He will serve you for ever. He will serve you here in this temple.'

She was so wrapped up in her prayers that she didn't hear Eli approaching. People came day after day to the temple, but it was rare to see someone pray like this. Hannah's lips were moving but no words were coming out of her mouth; she was simply crying out to God from her heart.

Eli interrupted her. 'Are you all right?' he asked. 'Have you been drinking too much wine? Maybe you should go home.'

Hannah shook her head. 'I'm not drunk,' she reassured him. 'I just desperately want God to answer my prayer.'

Eli looked at the tear-stained face of the lady before him and knew that this time God would answer.

'Go, my child,' he said. 'May God give you what you have asked for.'

Hannah stood up. No longer did she feel sad. She knew God had heard her. She knew her wait was over.

The family returned home to Ramah and soon Hannah found out that she was going to have a baby. She couldn't contain her joy! She smiled and sang as she carried out even the most boring of jobs. Elkanah watched her, delighted that at last she was happy.

The baby was born and they called him Samuel, which meant 'heard by God'. Hannah picked the name because she always wanted to remember that God had listened to her cry for a child.

Hannah loved Samuel very much. Each day, she would wake with happiness in her heart as she looked down at his tiny face. She knew she had to make the most of every moment, for he would only be with her for a short time. She had made a promise to God and, no matter how hard it would be, she was determined to keep it.

For about three years, Hannah stayed at home with Samuel and didn't go up to the temple. At the end of that time, she knew Samuel was old enough to travel and he no longer needed the milk she provided. She had worked hard to prepare him for this day. From when he was tiny he had been told that soon he would go to the temple to live with Eli the priest and to learn how to serve God there. Now it was time for him to leave, Hannah felt she could burst with sorrow—but she also knew that this was the reason why Samuel had been born.

The journey to Shiloh seemed to pass too quickly and soon the temple was in sight. Hannah's heart felt as if it would break. There was Eli, looking older than the last time they met. She took Samuel carefully by the hand.

'Eli's there,' she whispered to him. 'That's Eli. Soon you will live with him.'

She purposefully walked over to the old priest.

'Do you remember me?' she asked. 'You once saw me crying out to God in this temple. I asked God for a son.'

She moved Samuel forward. 'God granted my prayer,' she continued. 'And now, as I promised, I give him back to you.'

Samuel moved towards Eli. Already, it was obvious that he felt at home in the temple. Suddenly, Hannah knew that she could cope with the separation from her son. She knew God was pleased that she had kept her promise. She knelt down and prayed, not a miserable prayer complaining about leaving her son at the temple, but a prayer of praise to the God who had given her this special gift.

Life back in Ramah felt different without Samuel, but soon Hannah found out that she was expecting another baby. Over time, she had three sons and two daughters, but Samuel was always in her thoughts. Each year, she would go up to the temple to visit him, taking with her a special coat she had made for him to wear. Each year, she marvelled at how quickly he had grown and how well he had adapted to life in the temple. Before long, he became a man, a man recognized by all those around him as a prophet sent from God. He became famous throughout the land—but to Hannah, he was always her special son Samuel, a precious gift of a child.

Samuel went on to become a great prophet among the people of Israel. We don't know much more about his mother. What would have happened if Hannah had given up asking God for a child? What would have happened if she hadn't kept her promise and handed Samuel over to Eli to serve God in the temple? We will never know the answer to these questions, but we do know that Hannah is a great example for us to follow. Sometimes we can feel that our problems are too small or even too big for God to be interested. Sometimes when we pray it feels as if God isn't listening at all. Hannah shows us that we must

never give up praying, because God always listens and
always understands.

What do you think?

1. Why do you think God allowed Hannah to have more
    children after Samuel had gone to live in the temple?

2. Read 1 Samuel 7:15–17. Samuel went to the temple
    at an early age, but did he ever forget his family and
    where he came from?

3. What does the story of Hannah teach us about prayer?

A best friend
The story of Jonathan

6

*(This story is based on
1 Samuel 14:1–14;
18:1–4; chapter 20;
and 2 Samuel chapter 9.)*

Jonathan waited nervously for his father to arrive. It was time for the New Moon celebration, and anyone of any importance was expected to attend the palace for the feast. Any minute now, the usual fanfare of trumpets would announce the arrival of the king of Israel, King Saul. When he was young, Jonathan had always imagined that one day those trumpets would sound for him, that one day he would replace his father as king. Saul still thought that would happen, but Jonathan knew differently!

He went over the plan again in his mind. His father would be furious if he ever found out. He must never know; Jonathan knew more than most how dangerous King Saul could be when he was angry.

The trumpets sounded, the king arrived, the guests were seated. Then there was a short lull before food would be served.

Jonathan's thoughts drifted to his friend, even now hiding in a field not far from the palace. It was so many years since he and David had first met. He remembered David's arrival at the palace, when he had looked so scared and out of place, carrying only a harp in his hands. Jonathan would sometimes sit and listen while David played for King Saul. Sometimes, the two of them would talk, but their worlds seemed to have little in common: Jonathan was the son of a king, and David was a simple shepherd-boy from Bethlehem. No one would have guessed then that years later they would have become so close, more like brothers than friends.

It was David's first meeting with the Philistine army that seemed to knit the two of them together.

Jonathan was a good soldier. He smiled as he

remembered David's face when he had told him about his first battle with their old enemies, the Philistines. He had sneaked out of the Israelite camp with his servant and tricked the Philistine army into believing that the Israelites were mounting a serious attack. The Philistines had all turned and run away. King Saul and the army of Israel had been stunned; they hadn't even noticed that Jonathan and his servant were missing! However, that defeat was nothing compared with David's triumph!

Once again, the Israelites and the Philistines had been at war, but this time there was a major problem. Each day, a huge Philistine called Goliath marched towards the Israelites, shouting for someone to be brave enough to fight him. Each day, the soldiers had run away, terrified. This happened for forty days! That was when David had arrived. He was very young, but he couldn't understand why any Israelite was frightened when God was on their side. So he fought Goliath and won, with one tiny stone—one stone and the power of the living God. It was then that Jonathan realized that God was with David in a special way. It was then that he realized that one day it would be David who became king, not him.

The strange thing was that he wasn't jealous—he was actually glad. He even made a pact with David, promising that he would support David in battles and protect him as long as he lived. In return, David had promised to look after Jonathan's family for the rest of his life.

Jonathan's thoughts were interrupted as the food began to be served. He could see Saul was looking around, his eyes searching the crowds that were gathered. He knew the question would soon be asked.

So much had happened since that first realization that God's plan for his life was different from that made by his father. Many battles had been fought and won, and David had become the most famous fighter in Israel. Wherever David went, it seemed that crowds would cheer and chant his name. It was hardly surprising that King Saul was incredibly jealous. But to try to kill David because of it! Jonathan couldn't stand by and let that happen. He had protected David many times in the past; he would do the same again now.

'Jonathan,' his father spoke quietly as if he had something to hide, 'where is David? This is the second day of the feast, and I expected him to be here.'

Jonathan took a deep breath. This was it, the start of the plan.

'Father, David begged me to let him go away on urgent business,' he replied. 'I said he could go. It was something to do with his family.'

What would Saul's reaction be? He and David had discussed this a few days beforehand. David was convinced that Saul was going to kill him; Jonathan thought he was wrong. It was then that they had hatched their plan. David would hide in a nearby field and would not go to the feast. When Saul noticed David was missing, Jonathan would say he was away on urgent business. If Saul didn't seem to be too bothered, it was unlikely that he had any intention of killing David; but if Saul lost his temper, then David would have to run away for ever.

So Jonathan waited.

Saul stood up. His face was going red. 'Get him!' he roared. 'Go and find him, and bring him to me!'

'But why?' asked Jonathan bravely. 'Why do you want to kill him? What has he done wrong?'

King Saul was so angry that he picked up a spear leaning against the wall and hurled it at Jonathan. Jonathan dodged out of the way. He was furious! He would not eat with a man who wanted to kill the future king of Israel. He stormed out of the room.

Jonathan wanted to go and find David immediately, but he waited until morning to put their plan into action. He knew his father might have arranged for him to be watched. Early in the morning, he took his bow and arrows and a small servant-boy and hurried to the field where David was hiding. Quickly, he fired three of his arrows and sent the boy to find them. As the boy ran to look for them, Jonathan shouted loudly, 'The arrows are beyond you!'

From his hiding-place, David heard the words. He knew that this was the signal they had chosen. Now he would have to run for his life.

Jonathan waited for the boy to collect the arrows and ordered him to return to the palace. He glanced around to make sure he wasn't being followed and then ran towards David. As soon as David saw Jonathan approach, he bowed down, his face to the ground. He might be the future king of Israel, but he knew that he owed his life to Jonathan, and he would be grateful for ever.

The two friends looked at each other. They knew they might never see each other again. From now on, Saul would order soldiers to watch Jonathan closely, in the hope that he would lead them to David. David would have to remain in hiding.

'You must go as fast as you can,' Jonathan ordered.

'My father wants to harm you, but I believe you are God's chosen king. You will always be my special friend; I will always try to protect you.'

'And I,' David promised, 'will look after your family as long as I live.'

The two men hugged each other. It was hard to say goodbye when they had been such close friends. Both men were great soldiers, leaders in battle, yet they both cried as they parted, especially David.

'Thank you,' he whispered. 'I will keep my word.'

Jonathan went back sadly to the palace. He might never see David again, but he had played his part in God's plan. He had protected the future king. It was some years before David was crowned king of Israel but, when that happened, David kept his promise to Jonathan and looked after all his surviving family.

Jonathan is one of the Bible's hidden heroes. He could have been jealous of David; after all, he should have been the next king, following his father, Saul. However, Jonathan was willing to accept God's plan for his life, even if it meant him becoming less important and David becoming more important. Jonathan was a true friend. When we are young, we can often think we would like to be rich and famous like David. However, the story of Jonathan shows us that God often has unusual and unexpected plans for our lives. Like Jonathan, we must be willing to do what God wants, even if it doesn't seem as glamorous or as important as what he asks other people to do.

What do you think?

1. How did Jonathan show that he was a good friend
    to David?

2. Look at 1 Samuel 23:16–18. Did Jonathan and David
    ever meet again?

3. Jonathan had a son called Mephibosheth. Read
    2 Samuel 4:4 to see what happened to him.

4. Read 2 Samuel 9:13 to see if David kept his promise to
    Jonathan about his family.

Quick action!
The story of Abigail

7

*(This story is based on
1 Samuel chapter 25.)*

Abigail heard the sound of heavy footsteps and looked up to see one of the servants running towards her.

'Mistress,' the servant gasped, 'Mistress, I'm sorry to disturb you, but you've got to do something, otherwise none of us will survive!'

'What is it?' asked Abigail. 'Quickly tell me what's happened.'

'It's your husband, Nabal,' said the servant, still panting for breath. 'You know how David and his followers have been camping in the Desert of Maon, quite close to where Nabal grazes his sheep?'

Abigail nodded.

'Well, David and his men have been so good to us over the past few months. They've protected us all the time. No one has ever dared steal any of our flocks because David and his men have been like a wall around us. They've guarded our sheep and us the whole time, even during the night.'

Abigail smiled. She had heard about David's actions and felt privileged that he should show such care for her family's belongings; he was a good man. She was certain that David was God's choice for the future king of Israel, although others, including her husband, Nabal, didn't seem to believe it.

'Go on,' Abigail encouraged the servant. 'Why are you so worried?'

The servant shook his head despairingly. 'Well, we were just with Nabal, helping him shear the sheep,' he continued. 'We looked up and saw ten of David's followers coming towards us. They said that David had sent them to ask Nabal for some food, with it being the special sheep-shearing season and with all the parties going on to celebrate.'

'And?' asked Abigail.

'Well,' said the servant nervously, 'Nabal said, "No!" Worse than that, he said loads of rude things about David and sent the men back to the caves with nothing. David will be furious!'

Abigail looked horrified. She knew that Nabal was a silly, selfish man, but this had to be the craziest thing he had ever done. Everyone knew that if you helped defend someone's land you had a right to be paid with food or provisions, especially at festival times. David would be so insulted and angry he would surely march down to destroy the whole of her family!

Abigail knew there was no time to lose.

'Quick,' she ordered the servants, 'don't let anyone tell Nabal. Bring me 200 loaves of bread, 100 raisin cakes, 200 fig cakes, some corn, some wine and some sheep. Get them as fast as you can and load what you can on to donkeys. As soon as you are ready, set off, and I'll follow you on my donkey. Hopefully, we can sort this out with David before he does something he will regret for ever.'

The servants obeyed her immediately. They knew that if anyone could sort this mess out it was Abigail. She had rescued her husband from so many difficulties in the years of their marriage! None of them had ever understood how a beautiful, intelligent woman like her could be married to such a dreadful man.

As fast as they could, Abigail and her servants headed towards the mountain caves. The ground was rough and treacherous. In places, huge boulders blocked the pathway, making it hard for the donkeys to get through and providing safe hiding-places for robbers. Mountains towered above them, throwing cold, dark shadows into the valleys. This was not the kind of place you would want to travel to alone. At times Abigail felt terrified, but she knew that this was the only hope if her family was to be saved.

After some time, the path led Abigail between two mountains and into a deep ravine. The dimness of the light and the chilliness of the air made Abigail shudder, but when she lifted her eyes to the mountainside and saw David and 400 of his men approaching, her heart began to pound loudly in her chest. She knew that the next few minutes were vital!

Quickly Abigail climbed off her donkey and walked towards David. As soon as they met she fell on the ground at his feet.

'Please listen to me,' she begged. 'My husband Nabal is a silly man. I didn't know you had asked for food, otherwise I would have sent it immediately. Look, here are my servants with plenty of food for you and all your men. Please, David, don't attack my family just because Nabal has done something wrong. If you do, then, when you are king, you will forever regret harming innocent people just because you were angry. Please just stop for a moment and rethink what you are about to do. Please keep my family safe.'

David looked down at Abigail still kneeling before him on the ground. She was right! As soon as he had heard that Nabal had refused to send food he had been so angry that he had left 200 men to guard their caves and set off immediately, with the rest of his men, to destroy Nabal's

land. As he gazed into Abigail's pleading eyes, he realized
that his anger had got the better of him. Why should
innocent men, women and children be harmed just because
of the actions of one man? Suddenly David felt his anger
slip away and he felt slightly ashamed.

'Get up,' he said gently to Abigail. 'I thank God that you
came to me today. You have stopped me doing something
that would have been wrong. I will accept your gifts, and
I promise I will not harm your family in any way. Now go
home in peace.'

Gratefully Abigail headed home with her servants.
When she arrived, Nabal was in the middle of a party with
his friends. She knew it would be no use talking to him
straight away, so she went to sleep.

When morning came, Abigail went and found Nabal
and explained exactly what she had done the previous day.
Nabal was so shocked when he realized that David had
been on his way to destroy everything he owned that he
collapsed, and ten days later he died.

As soon as David heard that Nabal had died he sent
a message asking if Abigail would become his wife. He
liked the idea of having such a brave, intelligent, beautiful
lady at his side when he became king! Abigail agreed, and
immediately she got back on her donkey and went to meet
David. They were married soon afterwards.

Most people have heard about the great King David who
fought against the giant Goliath and was used by God in
all sorts of amazing ways. However, not many people have

heard of Abigail. Abigail is one of the Bible's hidden heroes. She was willing to risk her life for the sake of her family. She showed wisdom and great courage and, thanks to Abigail, her family was saved from disaster. Abigail could have stayed at home and done nothing. She could have run away to escape from David. Instead, she went straight to the problem and did what she could to sort it out. Even when we are young there are times when we have to be brave, like Abigail, and stand up against things we know to be wrong. We need to remember that God can give us courage in any situation and that he promises always to be with us.

What do you think?

1. Why do you think the servants went to tell Abigail what her husband, Nabal, had done?

2. David was hiding from King Saul in the caves. David wrote Psalm 57 while he was hiding there. Have a look at verse 4 to see how he felt. Now have a look at verses 9, 10 and 11 to find out what he did when he was afraid.

3. Is there anything you need to be brave about at the moment? Ask God to help you.

A home of his own

The story of Elisha and the Shunammite lady

8

*(This story is based on
2 Kings 4:8–37.)*

Elisha struggled over the rocky ground until at last he saw the lights of the village flickering in the distance. He was nearly there! It wasn't easy being one of God's prophets. Of course, there were some highlights, like performing amazing miracles and hearing directly from God, but it was often a lonely life, wandering from place to place with nowhere to call home. That's why he always looked forward to his visits to Shunem.

He walked slowly towards the familiar house and smiled as he remembered his first visit there. It had been late in the evening, and he had been wondering where he could find some food, when suddenly a well-dressed lady appeared and begged him to come and eat with her and her husband. It was the start of a special friendship, and now, whenever Elisha was in this area, he knew there would be a meal waiting for him at their home.

He lifted a weary hand and banged on the door. Inside, there was a flurry of activity and the door opened, sending out a welcoming beam of light.

'Our great friend Elisha,' said an elderly lady. 'It's good to see you!'

'It's good to be here,' replied Elisha. 'I will never forget your kindness in feeding me.'

The lady ushered him inside and gently closed the door. 'You're always welcome,' she said gently. 'We are honoured to have a man of God in our home.'

Her wrinkled face broke into a broad smile. 'And today,' she continued, 'we have a surprise!'

'Indeed we do,' spoke a deep voice, as an elderly man walked into the room and hugged Elisha. 'My wife's idea.' He gazed at her lovingly. 'Come on, we'll show you before we eat.'

The man slowly led Elisha up the stairs and out onto the flat roof of the house. Elisha had been on the roof many times before. Often in the evenings, the three of them would sit talking and eating, looking up at the beautiful night sky and remembering the God who had made it all. However, today things looked different. A small new building stood proudly in one corner, and the lady took Elisha by the hand and led him towards it.

'Open the door,' she whispered. 'Go inside.'

Puzzled, Elisha did as he was instructed. He found himself standing in a small, cosy room. It was simply decorated, with a bed in one corner and a table and chair in another. A lamp flickering on the table filled the room with a warm glow.

'Do you like it?' asked the lady hopefully. 'We hope you do. It's yours.'

'Mine?' questioned Elisha.

The lady nodded. 'A room of your own,' she replied. 'Somewhere you can rest or pray or study. Somewhere you can call your home.'

Elisha looked into the smiling faces of his friends. He was speechless. Never before had someone shown him such love, such kindness. Somehow, the job of being a prophet and trailing all over the country following God's instructions would seem so much easier now that he had somewhere to come home to. He turned to his friends.

'Thank you,' he said quietly. 'I only hope that someday I can repay your kindness.'

Elisha loved his new room. At times, he would be away for many weeks, but the thought of returning to his friends and his own cosy room kept him cheerful. One day, as he was resting on his bed, an idea sprang into his mind. He called his servant, Gehazi, to him.

'Gehazi,' he said, 'my friends have been so kind building this room for me that I would love to do something for them. Have you any idea what I could do?'

Gehazi thought for a moment. 'They have no children,' he replied. 'They are getting old and I am sure they would love to have a son.'

Elisha liked the idea and talked to God about it. Then he asked the lady to come and see him. 'God has granted my request,' he told her. 'By this time next year, you will have a baby boy.'

Just as Elisha promised, the lady became pregnant and, before a year had passed, a son was born to the couple. Elisha now enjoyed his visits even more. He could hardly believe how quickly the little boy grew, and he loved to see him playing games and helping his father in the fields. For Elisha, it was the closest thing he had to a family.

As a prophet, Elisha spent a lot of time at a place called Mount Carmel. People would go to visit him there if they needed help or wanted to find out what God was saying to them in a certain situation. Mount Carmel was about fifteen miles from his new home. One day, when Elisha was visiting Mount Carmel, he looked up and saw his friend, the Shunammite lady, coming towards him on a donkey. Immediately he knew something must be wrong.

'Quick!' he shouted to Gehazi. 'Run down and ask her if she's all right. Ask her if her husband is all right, and ask her about the child.'

Gehazi ran as fast as he could, but the lady refused to tell him anything until they had met Elisha. As soon as they met, she fell down at Elisha's feet and began to sob.

'Why did you let me have a son if he was going to die?' she asked.

'Die?' said Elisha. 'Tell me about it—surely the boy's not dead!'

Between sobs the lady explained, 'My little boy was in the fields with his dad when suddenly he began to scream and hold his head. A servant carried him into the house and he clung to my knee all morning … but there was nothing we could do … he died just after noon.'

'So where is he now?' asked Elisha, pulling on his cloak.

'I hope you don't mind,' said the lady, 'but I carried him upstairs and laid him on the bed in your room. Then I climbed on the donkey and came straight to you.'

'Quick!' ordered Elisha to Gehazi. 'Take my staff and run to the boy. You will be quicker than I can be. If you meet anyone on the way, don't speak to them. Just get to the boy as fast as you can and lay my staff on top of the boy.'

'You'll come with us too, won't you?' begged the lady.

'Of course I'll come,' answered Elisha gently. 'But I'm not as young as I used to be. I'll hurry as fast as I can.'

When Elisha and the lady arrived at the house, Gehazi was waiting for them. He looked sad.

'It's no use,' he said quietly. 'I did what you said with your staff, but nothing happened.'

Elisha hurried upstairs to his room. There was the small boy, lying on the bed. Gently, he closed the door.

Gehazi and the lady waited patiently on the roof-top,

wondering what was going on inside the room. They could hear heavy footsteps walking backwards and forwards. Then, suddenly, they heard the sound of sneezing! It sounded like a child's sneezes, not like those of an old man.

'Aaaatishoo!'—one, two, three, four, five, six, seven times.

Then they heard Elisha's excited voice: 'Gehazi, go and get the lady of the house. Ask her to come here.'

Without waiting, the lady burst into the room. There, sitting up in bed, laughing and smiling, was her only son! The lady fell down at Elisha's feet.

'Thank you,' she whispered.

Elisha smiled. He was glad he had a God who could do such amazing things, but he was also very glad he had friends like these.

The Shunammite lady and her husband are not well-known Bible characters but they did a beautiful thing for Elisha. They are hidden heroes of the Bible. They used their money and their home in a way that made it easier for the prophet to get on with his job. If it had not been for their kindness, Elisha might never have had a real home, and they might never have had a son.

When we are young, it's easy to feel that there is not much we can do for God. This story teaches us that God values kindness very highly, and all of us have chances to be kind to other people day after day.

What do you think?

1. How do you think Elisha felt when he first saw his new
    room? How do you think the man and lady felt as they
    showed it to him?

2. Why do you think God allowed the boy to die?

3. Read 2 Kings 8:1–6. How else were the Shunammite
    lady and her husband repaid for the kindness they
    showed to Elisha?

Dare I speak?
The story of Naaman's servant

9

*(This story is based on 2 Kings chapter 5.
The Bible doesn't tell us the name of the
ladies in this story, but we are going
to call Naaman's wife Milcah and
the servant-girl Johanna.)*

Naaman gazed sadly into the eyes of his wife. They knew the time had arrived. They had kept their secret for long enough and now they had to face the truth.

'What are we going to do?' Milcah whispered softly, glancing at the large white patches that had appeared on Naaman's skin.

Naaman shrugged his shoulders. He had fought so many battles as commander of the Syrian army and was well known in the country for being a brave and fearless soldier, but now he felt terribly afraid.

'I don't know,' he answered quietly. 'I'll have to tell the king. There is no cure for leprosy; I may be like this for ever.'

It was a hard day. No matter how she tried, Milcah couldn't think of anything except the leprosy. In many places, people with leprosy were forced to live in colonies on the outskirts of towns, in order to make sure that the disease was not passed on to other people. She had seen them when she travelled, waving from a distance. These were men and women who had once lived happy lives with their families until the patches had begun to appear. Now they had little hope of ever returning home. She closed her eyes to try to block out the truth she wanted so badly to ignore: now this dreaded disease was in her home, and there was nothing they could do about it.

When she opened her eyes, she saw her servant, Johanna, watching her from across the room. She could tell from the look in Johanna's eyes that the servants had heard the news. She would never understand how servants always knew everything that went on in the household, even the best-kept secrets! Johanna had been hovering around her all day, asking if she needed anything and bringing her food and drinks, as if she really did care. Milcah had never understood that, either. How could Johanna always appear to be so happy? She was so far from her home.

Milcah's mind wandered back to the day Johanna had arrived in their house. She had looked so young, not old enough to be so far from her family. She had been taken captive in Israel and brought to Syria to be a slave for Commander Naaman's wife. It must have been awful for her, but she never complained, not even when the days were long and the work was hard. She would often sing songs from her homeland as she worked, and Milcah had often heard her discussing the God she worshipped with the other slaves from Israel.

Milcah smiled as Johanna approached her. She always knew when there was something Johanna wanted to discuss with her owner.

'What is it, Johanna?' Milcah asked softly.

Johanna swallowed hard. Usually, she would only ask her mistress how much food to buy at the market or what she would like to eat for the evening meal. But today she had something different to say, and she wasn't sure what her mistress would think.

'Please don't think I'm rude,' said Johanna shyly, 'it's just that I heard about your husband ...' Her words trailed off.

'Yes,' said Milcah, encouraging her to continue. 'You know about Naaman. I'm sure everyone will know soon.'

'It's just ...' Johanna fought for words. 'It's just ... I know how my master Naaman could get better!' She blurted out the words. 'You know how I was brought here ... Well, where I come from, there is a prophet called Elisha ... If Naaman went to see him, I am sure my God would heal him. My God can do all things.'

Milcah was quiet for a moment. In Syria, they didn't believe in this God that many of the servants talked about. However, there was something about Johanna. Something about the way she lived. Something about the confidence with which she spoke. What if she were right? What if there really was a God in heaven who could cure Naaman's leprosy? Surely they would be foolish not to try.

'Thank you, Johanna,' she said softly. 'I will talk to Naaman about what you have told me.'

Naaman and Milcah spent most of the night discussing what Johanna had said. To follow the suggestion of a slave seemed a strange thing to do, but they were desperate. Eventually, they made a decision. In the morning, Naaman got up and went straight to the palace of the Syrian king, where he explained everything that Johanna had told them.

'You must go immediately,' the king agreed. 'You are my best commander. I will do everything I can to help you get better.'

When Naaman arrived at the home of Elisha the prophet, a servant came out to meet him. Naaman was cross. He had come all the way from Syria and the prophet didn't even come out of his home to meet him personally! Didn't Elisha realize what an important commander he was? Here he was with horses and chariots, and the only person to greet him was a servant! He felt like going home!

The servant came forward. He obviously wanted to speak.

'Elisha says, "Go and wash seven times in the river Jordan and you will be healed of your leprosy!"' the servant announced.

Naaman was furious. As if it wasn't enough that his slave-girl had sent him here and only a servant had come out to greet him; now he was being sent to wash in the dirty waters of the river Jordan!

Naaman thought of all the beautiful, clean waters in Syria. Surely he could have washed in those! He stormed off in a rage.

After a few minutes, Naaman began to calm down. He looked again at the white patches spreading over his arms. He thought of the look on Johanna's face when she had told him that Elisha could heal him. She had believed it. That little slave-girl, so far from home yet still trusting in her God. He turned around to see another of his servants waiting to speak to him.

'My Lord,' the man said bravely, 'if the prophet had asked you to do something great, would you not have done it? Why not wash in the Jordan?'

Naaman knew the servant was right. It had to be worth a try. So he went down to the Jordan and dipped himself into the water seven times, as Elisha had told him to. When he came out, his skin was so soft and clean it could have belonged to a young boy! He was healed!

Naaman examined every bit of his body. There was not a trace of leprosy anywhere!

Immediately, Naaman went to say 'thank you' to Elisha.

'Now I know that there is no God in the world but your God,' he announced. 'From now on, I will follow him for ever.'

The Bible doesn't tell us anything else about Naaman. We assume that he returned to Syria a healed and changed man. Both Naaman's wife and Johanna must have been delighted to welcome him home and hear him speak about the God who can do anything.

When Johanna was captured and taken to be a slave in Syria, it must have felt as if her life was over. However, she didn't moan and complain; she got on with her work in a strange land but always remembered the God she had been taught about when she was very small. It was brave of Johanna to make the suggestion that Naaman should visit Elisha to be healed. It never occurred to her that he might not be healed. She trusted that God would never let her down. Johanna is one of the Bible's hidden heroes. She did the little she could do and it had a huge effect on Naaman's life. As children, we may feel that there is little we can do for God. This story reminds us that we can do and say small things that can have enormous effects when God uses them.

What do you think?

1. How do you think Johanna felt as she thought about telling her mistress about Elisha the prophet?

2. Why do you think Elisha didn't come out to greet Naaman?

3. What do you think Naaman's thoughts were when he came out of the river Jordan the seventh time?

4. What do you imagine was the first thing Naaman said to his slave-girl when he arrived home?

The singing army
The story of King Jehoshaphat

10

(This story is based on 2 Chronicles chapters 17–20.)

King Jehoshaphat sat back on his throne and sighed. It was rare that he ever had a few minutes of peace to stop and think, without servants or soldiers demanding his attention. He knew that being a king was a great privilege, but it certainly kept him busy! At least he had been set a good example by his father.

Jehoshaphat smiled sadly when he thought of King Asa. Overall, he had been a good king, but it was a shame that he had lost some of his trust in God towards the end of his life. Even now Jehoshaphat wondered whether God would have healed the terrible disease in Asa's feet if only Asa had been willing to ask him. It had been hard to see his father crippled for the last two years of his life; the doctors could do nothing to help.

Jehoshaphat blinked and pulled himself back from his thoughts into the real world. That was all a long time ago! He had been the king for many years now. He hoped that he was doing a good job. From the start his aim had been to lead the people in a way that would please God. As soon as he had become king he had ordered that all the idols and altars to false gods should be pulled down and that everyone should turn back to the one true God, who had done so much for his people in the past. He had chosen men to go to each town in the land of Judah, to read the Book of the Law that contained all the teaching that God had given to Moses many years before. As a result many people had turned back to following God and there had been peace in the land.

Through the open window Jehoshaphat could hear the sound of marching in the courtyard. He knew that God was responsible for the peace they had enjoyed in recent years, but he also knew that having such a strong army discouraged any enemies from attacking Judah. As soon as he had become king, Jehoshaphat had started to strengthen all the towns in the area. He had ordered that huge forts be constructed and that strong, fortified walls be built around each city. He had trained up vast armies and placed them in each town, and ordered that enormous stores be built to provide food should there be a time of famine.

Jehoshaphat gazed around the throne room in which he was seated. He had become both rich and famous. Stunning mosaics covered the floors and many of the walls were overlaid with gold. Beautiful purple cloths were draped at intervals around the room, giving a warm, luxurious feel. The room was full of ornately carved furniture with gifts from distant lands carefully arranged to show that the king was respected by all the surrounding countries. Jehoshaphat picked up one of the silver and gold goblets that a group of Philistines had presented to him during a visit to Jerusalem only a few days before. He wandered over to the window and smiled as he gazed out at the distant hills scattered with sheep and goats. He chortled to himself as he remembered the day some visiting Arabs had delivered more than 15,000 animals as a present to him. It had been a generous gift, but he had needed to employ extra herdsmen to cope with them!

Suddenly, the peace in the palace was shattered by the sound of shouting and the pounding of running feet. The worried face of one of Jehoshaphat's trusted servants appeared at the door.

'Your Majesty,' the servant said quickly, bowing to the floor, 'we have some visitors and they bring us bad news.'

'Show them in,' Jehoshaphat ordered.

The visitors entered the throne room and bowed down before the king.

'Your Majesty,' they said, 'we bring news that a huge army is heading towards Jerusalem. It is made up of men from many of the surrounding countries and it is going to attack Jerusalem first and then move on to take over the whole of Judah. The army has already been formed and it is marching towards Jerusalem as we speak!'

Jehoshaphat was horrified. If what these men were saying was true, he wouldn't have time to move soldiers from other cities before the enemies arrived. He had purposely kept a large group of soldiers in Jerusalem just in case something like this happened, but surely they wouldn't be strong enough against such a huge army; they would be heavily outnumbered.

Jehoshaphat knew there was only one thing to do. Quickly he sent messengers to every town in Judah telling the people to call out to God for help. He asked representatives from each town to travel to Jerusalem so they could all pray together and seek what God wanted them to do. Immediately everyone did what Jehoshaphat asked. Men and women, boys and girls, even babies gathered outside the temple. King Jehoshaphat stood up.

'Lord,' he prayed in a loud voice, 'you made the heavens and the earth. You are so powerful that no one can stand against you. Everyone in the surrounding countries knows that we follow you and that you protect us. In the past we didn't invade these countries because you told us not to, but now they are attacking us and we are so small compared with them, we have no chance against such a big army. Lord, we don't know what to do. Please help us!'

All the people waited in silence. Suddenly there was a noise in the crowd. A young man made his way forward; Jehoshaphat recognized him to be the prophet Jahaziel.

'God has given me a message for all of you gathered here today,' Jahaziel announced in a loud voice. 'God says we must not be afraid of such a huge army. The battle is not ours; it is his! God wants us to march out towards the enemy lines as if we were going to fight, but he promises that we will have to do nothing except watch, as he will fight for us!'

Immediately Jehoshaphat knew that this really was a message from God. He bowed down with his face to the floor in front of all the people, thanking and praising God for caring for them. All the people joined him.

The next morning, as the army gathered, Jehoshaphat ordered a choir of men to stand in front of the soldiers. As they began to march forward Jehoshaphat gave the command and the men began to sing, praising God for his goodness and thanking him for his love. As Jehoshaphat's army got closer to the enemy lines the attacking armies became confused about what was happening and began to fight among themselves! By the time Jehoshaphat and his men arrived at the battleground the fight was over; the enemies had defeated one another. The army from Judah didn't even raise a sword; none of their people were harmed in any way.

With great joy Jehoshaphat led all the men of Judah back to Jerusalem. They went immediately to the temple to worship God. There was a great party!

News about Jehoshaphat's great defeat of his enemies

spread through all the surrounding countries. Everyone who heard about it realized that it was no use fighting against a country that had God on its side. For the rest of Jehoshaphat's reign as king there was peace in Judah and Jehoshaphat continued to follow his God.

Most people have never heard of King Jehoshaphat. He is one of the Bible's hidden heroes. He trusted God even in the face of great danger, and he saw the importance of worshipping and praising God. When he got into difficulty he didn't try to work things out by himself but immediately prayed to God for help. Even when we are young, we sometimes find ourselves in difficult situations. King Jehoshaphat teaches us how important it is to talk to God about everything. This story also shows us the importance of worshipping God and how no situation is ever too hard for God to handle.

What do you think?

1. What do you think would have happened if King Jehoshaphat had gone out to fight the attacking armies without asking God what he should do?

2. Why do you think King Jehoshaphat became so rich?

3. What does this story teach us about prayer?

Adopted daughter
The story of Mordecai

11

*(This story is based on
the book of Esther.)*

Mordecai was worried. He remembered clearly the promise he had made to his uncle shortly before he died.

'Take care of Esther,' he had gasped. 'She is alone now. I give her into your care.'

Mordecai had welcomed his cousin into his home. He had provided for her and cared for her. He had taught her all the traditions of the Jewish people, just as his uncle would have wanted. He watched her now from across the room. She had grown into a beautiful young woman. That was one reason why it was so hard to let her go.

A loud knock on the door ended his thoughts. The time had come.

Gently, he kissed Esther on each cheek. 'May God be with you,' he said with a sigh. 'Remember all I have taught you. I will be close by. You must send a message whenever you need me.'

With great reluctance Mordecai opened the door and handed Esther over to the two guards who were waiting to take her away.

'Take good care of her,' he ordered. 'Goodbye, my child.'

He closed the door behind him. Already the house seemed quiet. So much had happened in the past few weeks. First, there had been all the trouble at the palace. He had been there at the start of it!

What a banquet it had been! King Xerxes had invited everyone who lived in Susa, from the most important person to the least. The palace was covered in drapes of blue and purple material. There were couches made of gold and silver, and the mosaic flooring was inset with costly stones. Mordecai had never seen anything like it in his life!

At the same time, Queen Vashti had also held a banquet to which all the women were invited. For much of the feast, King Xerxes had boasted about his beautiful wife, who was feasting with the women in a separate part of the palace. On day seven, he decided he wanted all the men to see her! So he sent servants to collect her.

'Tell her to put the royal crown on her head and appear here so that everyone will see how beautiful she is,' he commanded his servants.

Mordecai remembered the fearful faces of the servants as they returned without the queen.

'Where is she?' King Xerxes demanded. 'Where is my wife?'

'She won't come,' whispered the servants, trying to keep their answer secret from the silent room. 'She says she is staying where she is.'

Mordecai had never seen such anger. For the queen to disobey the king in private was one thing, but to embarrass him in public was too much for him to handle. Queen Vashti was banished from the palace for ever and would never see the king again.

There had been rumours all over Susa as to who the new queen would be. Everyone agreed that it wouldn't be long before King Xerxes sought a replacement for Vashti. Even so, when the announcement came, many were surprised. Servants were to be sent out all over the country to look for beautiful women. If any suitable women were found, they were to be taken to the palace for twelve months of beauty treatments. At the end of twelve months, the women would parade before the king and he would decide who should be his queen.

Mordecai laughed when he remembered the lengths to which women had gone in the hope that they would be noticed by the palace guards. His smile disappeared when he recalled the day he had noticed one of the guards watching Esther across the busy street. He had known immediately what would happen.

The summons to the palace had arrived the following day. Esther was allowed time to get herself ready and say her goodbyes. There was so much Mordecai needed to tell her in such a short space of time.

'Esther,' he had spoken with urgency, 'Esther, never forget you are a Jewish girl. Never forget the stories I told you about how God is always with us. But never tell anyone where you come from; keep it a secret, or you could be in danger.'

Esther had promised to do all that Mordecai had told her, and he knew that she would keep her promise.

Mordecai sighed. Life would be different now. He would have to care for her from a distance.

As soon as Esther arrived at the palace, her beauty treatments began. She was placed in the care of Hegai, who was to be in charge of all the girls who had been selected. From the start, Hegai seemed to take a special interest in Esther. She was somehow different from the other girls. She was always polite, never complained, and wasn't vain and conceited as some of the others were. Hegai made sure that she always got special treatment.

After twelve months, the time came for Esther to appear before the king. As soon as he saw her, he fell in love, and, before long, Esther was crowned as the new queen.

Every day now, Mordecai would travel to the palace and sit beside the king's gate. He wanted to be near Esther, close enough to help if she needed anything. One day, while he was there, Mordecai overheard two of King Xerxes' guards talking in hushed tones. As he listened, it became clear that they were planning to kill the king! Secretly, Mordecai sent a message to Esther to tell her of the plot. Immediately she warned the king. King Xerxes was so grateful that he asked his scribes to write in a book about how his life had been saved.

Soon after he had saved the life of the king, another problem arose for Mordecai. There was a man in Susa called Haman. King Xerxes was pleased with Haman and promoted him to be his second-in-command. Haman liked to feel important and ordered that all the people in the land should bow down to him whenever they were in his presence. Although not everyone was happy with the idea, all the people did as they were told; all, that is, apart from Mordecai. He was a Jew and he knew it was wrong to bow down and worship anyone other than God. Haman was furious with Mordecai and decided to find out more about him. When he discovered that Mordecai was a Jew, an evil plan began to form in his mind. Wouldn't it be great, he thought, to get rid of not just Mordecai, but all of the Jewish people?

Haman arranged to see King Xerxes. He told the king that the Jewish people scattered all over the province were the only ones who refused to obey all the king's laws. Then he made a suggestion.

'King Xerxes,' he said craftily, 'if the Jewish people don't always obey you, surely other people will see that and begin to disobey you too.'

King Xerxes thought about it for a moment. It certainly sounded likely.

'So,' Haman continued, 'why don't you make an order that all the Jews should be killed? I will even give you the money to pay the people who carry out your order.'

The king agreed with Haman and a message was sent out to all the surrounding areas, announcing that on a certain day all the Jewish people were to be killed. When Mordecai heard the news, he tore his clothes and began to cry. The same thing happened in all the other areas where the Jewish people lived; everyone was terrified.

When Esther heard that Mordecai was crying at the king's gate, she sent one of her servants to find out what the problem was. Mordecai sent a message back explaining that the lives of all the Jews—including her own life—were in danger. He asked her to go to King Xerxes and see if he would help. Now it was Esther's turn to be afraid. No one was allowed to go to see the king unless he sent for him or her first, and it was thirty days since he had last seen Esther. She sent a message to Mordecai.

'For the next three days, tell all the Jews to fast and pray. On the fourth day, I will risk my life and go to see the king. If I die, I die.'

Esther went to see the king and he was pleased to see her. He gave an order allowing the Jews to fight against anyone who tried to harm them. The Jews fought and won, and Haman was killed. More than that, the king discovered the book in which it was recorded that Mordecai had saved his life, and he promoted Mordecai to be his second-in-command and gave him all Haman's land and possessions. From his position of power, Mordecai was able to protect the Jews for the rest of his life, as well as always being there to watch over his cousin Esther.

Mordecai is one of the Bible's hidden heroes. Queen Esther would not have been in a position to save all those people if it hadn't been for her cousin Mordecai. If he had not taken her in when her father died, who knows what would have happened to her? As it was, he brought her up to understand that God can work in any situation and that nothing that happens to us is too bad or too difficult for God. Esther had to risk her life when she went to see the king, but it is unlikely she would have done so if Mordecai hadn't taught her about the amazing power of God.

What do you think?

1. Why do you think Mordecai tore his clothes and cried when he heard about the king's command?

2. What did Esther mean when she said, 'If I die, I die'?

3. What might have happened if Esther hadn't become queen?

To the rescue

The story of
Ebed-Melech

12

(This story is based on
Jeremiah 38:1–13 and 39:15–18.)

Ebed-Melech felt uneasy. As a well-respected slave in the palace of King Zedekiah, he was often present when important decisions were made, but over the years he had learned to keep quiet and pretend he hadn't heard! After all, he was only a slave. He had no right to an opinion. He had to work for the king without question, no matter what he was asked to do. Usually, the job was not too bad, but today it was different.

King Zedekiah was obviously worried. It had been such a relief, a few months ago, when the announcement was made that Pharaoh's army from Egypt was on its way to help defend Jerusalem against the Babylonians. The Babylonians had been far too frightened to do anything with the might of Egypt bearing down upon them! They had retreated, and Jerusalem had been left in peace. Now, however, the Egyptians had gone home, and the news had arrived that the Babylonian army was ready for another attack on the city. All the people were terrified, and already many had left Jerusalem and joined the Babylonians!

For many years now, Jeremiah, the prophet, had been predicting this war. Worse than that, he had prophesied that the Babylonians would easily defeat the Israelites, unless the Israelites turned back to following their God. But no one had taken any notice. Jeremiah had been beaten, banished from the land, even placed in prison, but still he wouldn't stop telling the people what God had told him to say.

The thing was that Ebed-Melech believed him. Maybe he was only a slave, but he had come to trust the God whom Jeremiah followed, although just now it felt as if he was the only one who did! Ebed-Melech couldn't help imagining

what would happen if the Babylonians attacked. Would all
the people he had worked for all these years be carried off
to Babylon and find themselves serving as slaves there?
Sometimes things had a funny way of turning around
in life!

A loud noise interrupted his thinking. Looking out of
the window, he saw Jeremiah being dragged across the
courtyard by a group of men. It looked as if they had at
last got what they wanted. He had heard them talking
to the king, although he wasn't certain what they were
planning to do. After a short while they returned, but
Jeremiah was not with them. Ebed-Melech could hear their
mocking voices.

'Well, that should be the end of him!'

'Did you hear him shout as he landed in the mud?'

'No one else will hear him shout—he's too far down to
be heard!'

'At least that will stop him telling lies!'

Ebed-Melech couldn't believe it. So that was their
decision! He had heard them suggest it. Jeremiah had been
thrown down the deep well in the courtyard of the king's
son. There was no escape from there. Everyone knew that
the well held no water; just thick, soft, squelchy mud lined
the bottom of it. He shook his head despairingly. He would
have to do something! He knew where the king was. He had
seen him sitting at the Gate of Benjamin.

Putting aside his fear, Ebed-Melech left the palace. As
a slave, he was not allowed to approach the king unless
he was sent for. His actions now would place his life in
danger, but he knew that if he didn't act quickly, Jeremiah
would die.

'My lord the king,' he said, bowing down to the ground, 'I know that earlier you handed Jeremiah over to your officials so they could do to him whatever they wanted, but I am begging you to think again. They have thrown him down a deep well, and if we don't rescue him soon, he will die. He is God's special prophet. We can't let this happen!'

Ebed-Melech paused and waited for the king's response. King Zedekiah was silent for a few minutes. He was tired of the constant moaning of his officials whenever Jeremiah began to speak, but, at the same time, Jeremiah was worrying all the people with his predictions that the Babylonians would win the war. It had been such a relief to hand him over to his officials; it had saved him thinking about what to do! But what if Jeremiah really was a messenger from God? What if the words he said were true and he, the king, had allowed him—even helped him—to be killed? He studied Ebed-Melech's face. It was certainly brave of him to speak out. Maybe he should take note of what this young slave said and follow his courageous example. Suddenly he made a decision.

'Quick!' he said. 'Take thirty men with you. Get him out before he dies!'

Ebed-Melech ran to the palace. He summoned the men and searched in a room under the palace for old clothes he could use as rags. Then, as fast as they could, the men raced towards the well and called down to Jeremiah. They heard a movement in the mud below. He was still alive!

Quickly, they tied the rags to the ends of ropes and lowered them down the well.

'Put the rags under your arms to pad the ropes,' shouted Ebed-Melech. 'We'll soon have you out!'

The men felt a tug on the rope and began to pull. Slowly, Jeremiah was lifted out of the well until he lay cold and muddy on the courtyard floor. He was safe!

King Zedekiah sent a message to all his officials, ordering that Jeremiah should be allowed to remain in the palace courtyard and that no harm was to come to him. Jeremiah was washed and given fresh clothes to wear.

Even after all that he had been through, Jeremiah continued to warn the people that, if they didn't turn back to God, the Babylonians would come and take over the land. Still no one, apart from Ebed-Melech, took any notice. One day, Jeremiah took Ebed-Melech to one side.

'Listen, Ebed-Melech,' he said, with a grateful look in his eyes, 'God spoke to me again last night. He told me that the Babylonians will attack Jerusalem very soon but that you have nothing to fear. God is going to keep you safe because you trust in him.'

Soon everything happened just as Jeremiah had predicted. The Babylonians attacked Jerusalem and many of the Israelites were taken back to Babylon as slaves. Jerusalem lay in ruins for about fifty years.

Just like Ebed-Melech, Jeremiah was also kept safe. King Nebuchadnezzar, the king of Babylon, had heard all about Jeremiah's prophecies and allowed him to live wherever he wanted in the land.

Many people have heard of the great prophet Jeremiah, but only a few have any idea who Ebed-Melech was, even though he saved the prophet's life! Ebed-Melech is one of the Bible's hidden heroes. He could easily have spent his life moaning about being a slave in a country over a thousand miles from home, but instead he did what he could from the position he was in. Not many of us will end up being famous like Jeremiah, but this story shows us clearly the importance of every person in the plans that God has. Wherever we are, whatever family we are in, God knows about it, and we are there for a very special reason!

What do you think?

1. What would have happened to Jeremiah if Ebed-Melech had not rescued him?

2. Read Jeremiah 39:16–18. How do you think Ebed-Melech felt when Jeremiah said this to him?

3. What lessons can we learn from Ebed-Melech's life?

About Day One:

Day One's threefold commitment:

~ To be faithful to the Bible, God's inerrant, infallible Word;

~ To be relevant to our modern generation;

~ To be excellent in our publication standards.

I continue to be thankful for the publications of Day One. They are biblical; they have sound theology; and they are relative to the issues at hand. The material is condensed and manageable while, at the same time, being complete—a challenging balance to find. We are happy in our ministry to make use of these excellent publications.
JOHN MACARTHUR, PASTOR-TEACHER,
GRACE COMMUNITY CHURCH, CALIFORNIA

It is a great encouragement to see Day One making such excellent progress. Their publications are always biblical, accessible and attractively produced, with no compromise on quality. Long may their progress continue and increase!
JOHN BLANCHARD, AUTHOR, EVANGELIST AND APOLOGIST

Visit our website for more information and to request a free catalogue of our books.

In the UK: www.dayone.co.uk

In North America: www.dayonebookstore.com

Twelve Hidden Heroes – New Testament

REBECCA PARKINSON

96PP, PAPERBACK

978-1-84625-211-2

Many people dream of becoming rich and
famous. We're fascinated by the people who
seem important, but often we don't notice those
who are working behind the scenes. Most of us
are familiar with the famous Bible stories from
the New Testament, but in this book Rebecca
Parkinson looks at some of these stories from
a different viewpoint, considering some of the
unnoticed characters who are rarely mentioned
but whose actions were used by God to make a
massive difference. This is a companion book to
Twelve Hidden Heroes: Old Testament.

Rebecca Parkinson lives in Lancashire with
her husband, Ted, and their two children. She
became a Christian after realizing that the Bible
isn't a boring old book, but a living book that is
full of exciting stories that still change people's
lives. A teacher and the leader of the youth
work in her church, she now loves to pass the
Bible stories on to others in a way that everyone
can understand.

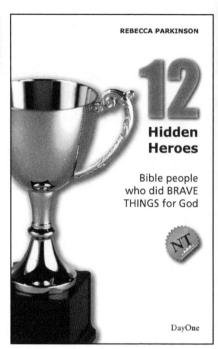

REBECCA PARKINSON

12
Hidden
Heroes

Bible people
who did BRAVE
THINGS for God

NT

DayOne